HANNAH AND THE HOLY FIRE

Hannah and the Holy Fire

Poems by

K. Louise Vincent

OOLICHAN BOOKS

LANTZVILLE, BRITISH COLUMBIA, CANADA

2003

National Library of Canada Cataloguing in Publication Data

Vincent, K. Louise (Karen Louise), 1956-

Hannah and the Holy fire / K. Louise Vincent.

Poems.

ISBN 0-88982-187-9

1. Refugees—Canada—Poetry. 2. Refugees—Bosnia and Hercegovina—
Poetry. I. Title.

PS8593.I4487H34 2003   C811'.6   C2003-906829-3

The Canada Council | Le Conseil des Arts
for the Arts | du Canada

We gratefully acknowledge the support of the Canada Council for the Arts for our publishing
program.

BRITISH
COLUMBIA
ARTS COUNCIL
Supported by the Province of British Columbia

Grateful acknowledgement is also made to the BC Ministry of Tourism, Small Business and
Culture for their financial support.

Canada

We acknowledge the financial support of the Government of Canada through the Book
Publishing Industry Development Program for our publishing activities.

Cover image from a painting by Wendy Skog.

Published by
Oolichan Books
P.O. Box 10, Lantzville
British Columbia, Canada
V0R 2H0

Printed in Canada

For anyone who longs for home

Acknowledgements

To the exquisite women of the Island Poets' Meeting so generous with their unabashed intelligence and humour, and the annual Glenairley Writer's Retreat with Patrick Lane—thank you all for sharing such love of the craft.

My appreciation to Marilyn Bowering for welcoming me into her course on narrative/serial poetry at Malaspina University-College when I was lonely for dialogue on the long poem.

Much love and gratitude to my family, particularly my mother, Alice Schmidt, and my compassionate cowboy, Bob McKecknie. And for my father's (the late Henry Schmidt) faith.

For their support and sight, I am thankful to Laurie Burns, Cindy O'Dell, Brenda Gaertner, Audrey Keating, Odette Laramee, Sandra Loschnig, Kit Pepper, Robert Pepper-Smith, Sylvia Raine, Deborah Schwartz and Joanne Thorvaldson.

I am indebted to the writers quoted in this book; their work keeps me open.

And finally, my gratitude to Ron Smith, Hiro Boga and Jay Connolly at Oolichan Books for providing such a fine home for Hannah.

Contents

1. Hannah

But this life of continuing is for the sane mad
and the bravest monsters.

—Adrienne Rich

All plants emit light and indeed all bodies do.

—Octovio Paz

Canada, 1996

i

There were many tattoo parlours for Hannah to choose from:
Temple Tattoos, Mom's Tattoos; The Devil's Den
business card read: *And Home For Wayward Young Ladies:*
tattoos pierced, virgins deflowered, prudes perverted,
fantasies fulfilled.. Hannah chooses Sacred Heart Tattoos;
like a convent she thinks. Death is advertised on the walls,
drawings of skulls and crosses, barbed-wire necklaces,
stark statements of mortality beside flowers, saints,
even the great OM. Beautiful and banal.
Hannah likes the no bullshit terms of the body.
Gut morality. She lights a cigarette and enters.

Inside a man with a silver braid down the length of his spine
sits beside her, quiet. *I'm not here for sex,*
Hannah begins. He smiles, *for a tattoo then.*
Looking closely at him she remembers
reading about the Harsavojoch ice-man,
the meridian of lines marked along his back and legs.
The 5,000 year old people found in the ice
were all tattooed. Perhaps acupuncture for pain,
perhaps prayer. Perhaps, the earliest form of art.
Four weeks later there it is, a small painting
needled in her skin. Her private canvas,
her meditation on memory, an angel-animal
sealed in the soft skin of her solar plexus.

ii

In the bright glare of morning Hannah
glides with wet feet into the garden.
Summer shines through her,
you can see it rise, a halo of green
evaporating the dark pool of her night body.

The moment her hand touches the ink-blue
pollen inside the vaginal fold of the poppy,
an electric shock explodes
in the base of her spine. She sees then
what tattoo will be stained next on her skin.

iii

Hannah goes back to the tattoo parlour. This time
there is no doubt. She already anticipates the needle,
the sudden surge as the skin comes alive,
the small rapture of being. She returns home
sore and elated, tells nobody. In a private celebration
she applies the alcohol with devotion, a marked angel
absorbing the red drops of her life.

A dispatch of memories presses through her dreams now.
The hardness of metal against her spine, the spit
of soldiers on her face and breasts, the shouting
in her ear. *You fucking gutasa you should be crushed
to the end.* The cries her mother makes
when Hannah crumples inside herself
and the light in her eyes darkens.

*Gutasa is a derogatory political term that refers to the fascist
regime in Croatia (then including Bosnia-Herzegovina) that
collaborated with Hitler. Siberian leaders used the term for
Muslim and Croatian women in rape camps. Most of these
women were not born until after WWII.*

iv

Hannah arrives with the past and future folded inside her
like an old letter about to disintegrate. A site of loss
and longing. Her third tattoo will be the simplest.
Inside his studio Armen waits, pared inward
by poverty, by the pulse of his art. He prays
for recovery, for the body to belong again.
When you survive torture and displacement,
he tells Hannah, *you carry the dead inside you.*
First and last occupants, they are imbedded
where pain lodges, they are not lost.
When you're born in a country to which it's impossible to return,
leaving lasts all your life. Pain is not knowing one's place,
the pleasure of arriving and knowing you are home.
When there is no centre, memory becomes home;
the fit of a doorknob in your hand, a room, a river,
a relative's final gift. Its shelter sits inside you.
Armen shows Hannah the story engraved on his chest,
his relief carvings, his clandestine cryptograms of faith.
When he removes his shirt, a solar system explodes
from the centre of his heart. Hannah counts
nine shades of ink, a galaxy of blue for every life
Armen loved and lost. Hannah tells him then,
I want my name, I want Hannah tattooed
here on my wrist where it won't be forgotten.

Canada, 1997, Hannah's Recipe for Ink

v

Begin with a pencil
and make a raft.
Go to graveyards
and wedding sites.
Go pot-luck, be hospitable.
Make room for strangers;
learn their names, the odour
of their origins.

Prepare to travel alone.
You might find yourself
at the beginning, late
at night, sprouting roots
from your fingers.
If you grow gills,
don't be alarmed.
Go deeper, swim
with the cuttlefish
in their cloud of sepia.

Drink indigo.
Mix an infusion.
Hand paint the earth
vermilion. Be hopeless.
A recipe for ink
is impossible to measure
when it's a question
of faith, seaweed
and fire.

Begin with a pencil,
and make a raft.
Draw a map. Remember
when you go down
to come back.

Canada, 1998

vi

We didn't descend from heaven; we descended from trees. Heaven, however, is in the trees and as Hannah presses her back in the bark of the giant fir, heaven is in her. She sees no-one for months and feels the hole in her heart fill with green and blue. She sleeps in a tent on sweetgrass and swims in the river that spills its insides into the sea. Hannah has gone as far as she can go. The end of earth, an edge, an island, sacred territory, Haida Gwaii—where the black bears are coming out of hibernation.

Hannah lies motionless, learning a quiet still as stone. At night, when the bear sniffs the corners of the tent, her heart pounds so hard she presses it down with both hands. The entire side of the tent leans inward as the swell of the bear curves against her. In the morning she moves from the new grass toward the trees where the ground is a scattering of salal and shard. Later, an amused watchman tells her that bears eat grass the first weeks after hibernation. *You are on their territory; they know it,* he says, *and need to know you know it.*

Exhausted, Hannah sleeps in a hammock slung close to the river. She wakes up as five bears wade by, black as the raven. When Hannah lowers her head in a quiet nod, they nod back, eyes shining. For three weeks Hannah stays on; each day visions of people appear. Visions of men and women cleaning fish, cooking and singing, smoke the air. Children play, laughter flows everywhere. She sees, but isn't seen. From then on, Hannah prays; if praying is staying in silence and letting it fill you like the land fills the bears.

When there is rest
let my mind be taken by trees
until it is no longer I
who thinks.

Let me climb into the boat of myself and wait
for songs, for birds who no longer sing,
whose nests disappeared when the green
hearts of trees were broken.

Let me dream of small brown birds,
yellow ones and blue; the red birds
and the black. When they sing
they each have a name and I know
the language to tell them mine.

Let me drift toward morning,
toward the delight birds bring
when eyes open again and see green.
Let me hear the peacock who never resists
proclaiming green can be worn
from the inside out. A skin
of leaves and feathers.

Green leaf, blue feather;
they are close. When they sleep
the trees relax and become
a bed of water.

viii

In the sleeping body of Hannah
is another sleeping body
and one who is wide open dreaming
and one who is crazy
and one who is educated
and therefore.
In the sleeping body of Hannah
is a poem just waking up.

2. Emily

It felt like we were at the bottom of a sacred river.
—Ben Okri

Some place past emptiness, we take another step.
—Jan Zwicky

Yugoslavia, 1994

ix

Emily is in Sarajevo, morning refuses to come, the sky stays a blackened yellow as she lies in her dress exhausted; now her legs hang down the bedside, a long pause before her body breaches upward, cold feet on a cold floor, the bathroom light blinding as she stares faceless in the mirror, washes, pulls back her hair, eyes blink, then blink again, nothing rests, Emily lies back down frozen, mothers lie awake in this country, that country, this war, that war, in the next room her daughter Hannah lies awake, eyes open, listening as morning comes slowly, soundless as an assassin.

Emily is thinking of other women wearing sweaters and socks like bandages while they gather remnants of the past and look for what can be salvaged and rebuilt; devastation spares nothing but the present, everything else is temporary; from her bed she watches the sky for signs; she is praying for the children she saw cradling guns larger than their arms, their small hearts the same size as their fists, opening and closing, while Emily waits, while Hannah waits, while a love that is shocking waits, like all love waits, for the night, the day, when this heart, that heart opens, indivisible.

x

Emily dreams she is really going
to see him again, to be with her husband.
He has made sure to find a room
with a bed and a bath, a refuge
after seven months. His eyes are the same
surprise she saw when she was fourteen,
earth, with the shock of sun at noon.
Emily feels light, a blue boat floating.
He locates each vertebra of her spine,
a bridge of river stones under his tongue.
He licks her belly until it shines
and swells like a moon.
He touches and turns her until
the sweet river waiting inside her breaks
and a combustion of absence weeps.

xi

When her body lies down tired and grateful for sleep, a gate slowly closes; the mind pulls down the black blind and the gift of stillness circles until the first moment of sleep when a horse bursts out and the body jumps awake. Every time it is like this, the night blind snaps open and a wild horse breaks the lead line held for a second just right.

xii

Emily dreams the assassin's identity;
His heart rests in his hands
with the wounds of her daughter
and the death of her husband.

England, 1996

xiii

They listen to Charlie Parker
in a temporary apartment in London
when they meet Leda
and simultaneously fall in love—
Parker's music a language for confusion
and complexity to live together,
a democracy of emotion
and improvisation—the words they speak later
are simple and sincere:
let's live together and see
what weather will come and go,
what keys will open what doors.

Canada, 1996

xiv

They live now, safely
on the west coast where
everything is washed
fresh by the rain and where
everything grows.

It isn't the first time they find themselves alone and speechless. For Emily, silence is the second skin of an animal healing an invisible wound. Silence is as familiar as her own scent, the scent of night. Emily is like an animal that has fed itself for so long on nothing, the memory of food has no smell left. For Emily, silence is existence.

For Leda aloneness is like encountering an animal in the wilderness. Leda doesn't want to know the nature of this silence; her life stops when language ceases and human companions disappear. Time with Emily is different; it asks for patience, the quiet waiting in the time-less life of a bear living in an old forest.

They sit in the darkening room. They have been there since late afternoon. It is close to six o'clock and the light is leaving like a guest feeling the pull of home. Edges and colour fade; body shapes soften. Leda doesn't want this time with Emily to end. Blue eyes looking into brown ones; sky soaking into earth.

How do I know Hannah is alive? Emily asks. *Maybe she is still here, in this room, wondering what room to go into next. Do you remember what she said before she left? She said, —I am going somewhere new and I am already there; I am only waiting for the blindfold to drop from my eyes. I feel Hannah is waiting for us to see something new.*

xvi

Emily pushes a canoe into the water
bends her body slowly
lifts the paddles
folds her arms like woollen wings
and glides away

Around the point past the reef
where seagulls sit in a well-rehearsed chorus line
Emily's second self stands
pinned
between the moon and sun
pinned like fabric on fabric
pressed like frost on window
pale blue layers of light
joined seamlessly

She remembers her dream
a translucent seahorse spinning
vertically
through miles of salt chuck
a torpedo of startled flesh
falling

She remembers the dream
ruptured, the phone ringing
then pulling her from sleep, a stranger
asking *is this Emily, I am sorry*
to have to tell you

Inside the cove moss grows
on grey heads of stone, a house
stands empty in the distance
inert eagles sit transfixed in green
triangular towers, they are watching
the sea swell, the shoreline
disappear

When Emily comes back from her paddle she sits at the table by the window, watching morning seep into the kitchen. Leda reaches for the kettle. *Tea?* she asks. Emily nods her head and while Leda pours she has a vision of Emily as a young girl in a boat. Handing the cup to her, she notices the blue in Emily's eyes is as pale as ash. They sip and watch a small shroud of steam form on the window. Mint soothes their throats while they rest in complete silence. They wait until Emily speaks into the empty space: *there is a sound that silence makes and I am waiting for that. I need to hear Hannah's voice in that silence.*

On the sixth day of her vigil, Emily hears Hannah's voice. The moon is a white brighter than snow, a focused headlight searching. It has been another sleepless night and she decides finally to get up, dress and walk down to the water. Outside, a skin of frost has formed on the ground, telephone wires and trees. It is here, in the absolute stillness of the night, when she stands where the grass meets the beach and the sea sighs hard, that she hears her daughter say, *Mother, don't worry. I will write to you; I will write you letters when I can see again.*

Canada, 1997

xviii

Where are you now, Hannah?
I am here, fire in your body.
Where? On your tongue
as you twist loss into a language
you can hear the shape of, a tattoo
that heals itself by weeping.

How many times must we give birth to loneliness?
Each time a winter wind strips colour
leaf by leaf back to bone.
Each time language burns its alphabet
to ash. Loneliness finds its way back
one leaf at a time. When it does
it is not only astonished, it is grateful.

Who dreams the same dream?
Boat workers and water birds. Swimmers
dream of galaxies, astronauts hear the sea
pull like dry silk. Singers and glassblowers
dream the same dream. Builders of houses
dream what the house they are building
dreams.

xix

When you were born, Hannah, your father walked miles
through snow on bush roads from camp. We were lucky
he was home that year and sometimes working.
It was dark when he arrived at the hospital in Sarajevo.
He was soaked to the skin and singing. He was so happy
when he kissed me and I told him he had a daughter.

Yugoslavia, 1982

xx

Hannah, two years old, a green stem
winding and unwinding
in Emily's arms, a botanical beauty
holding her mother's face
between hands soft as leaves.

3. Leda

Feelings after all, belong to the angels. They are masters of intensity.
—Robert Hass

This gentleness we learn from what we cannot heal.
—Bronwen Wallace

Canada, 1998

xxi

After Hannah, then Emily, leaves, Leda moves into a trailer so small it could fit into most kitchens. She learns to pick up a brush under any circumstance, begin. One colour moving into another until a flame ignites the dry canvas and the wet particles alive in the paint take a breath, then burn.

Leda paints street angels that strut. They are a stigma, a presence wounded by time. They live the liberty of the abandoned who know inside out the daily dangers of surviving and dying. They are homeless angels, forgotten angels, free, naked, retrospective angels.

When they smile Leda knows Michelangelo's angels are not the only angels who fly, and who cross over, *who rise again in pure relation.** She paints the secret of all benevolent, bisexual, multi-lingual angels. She paints not the pain in the paint but the paradox.

* Robert Hass

Leda, her hands lost in the wheel, notices
the glaze on the vase by the window
is the same red as the dahlias
orphaned inside. Crimson bleeds on the front
as though the flowers themselves spilled
their heart's interior.

The wheel turns, its years betrayed by small moans.
As Leda presses the bowl empty she decides
to glaze this one cerulean blue. Its flesh crying
sea, sky, I am neither. Tears drip salt in the clay
as it becomes a dream for crimson singing
early in the morning garden.

Leda makes a wish, holding a small rib of a deer in her hand. When it snaps she is surprised the same way she was as a child holding a Christmas ornament, its fragile thinness frightening her the moment before she crushes it in the small nest of her hand.

Leda cuts the red thread circling her wrist since her friends left, winds it tight until the two pieces of bone are sealed. She finds a cord and hangs the bone around her neck. She returns to work now with the white, crescent scar curved in the hollow of her heart.

Canada, 1998

xxiv

Strange angels visited that Spring
when empty beds in the garden, her house
when everything waited, when no lovers
lay down, no heart, no earth opened
its dark soil, no hope flared wild like poppies
in unexpected places, they arrived red skin glowing
they watched the day, the night, the space between
They didn't know the length of time, it circled
it spun, when it turned inside out, they went smiling
in the garden, they planted the small seeds
they arranged a gentle order of growth, they sang
they carried water in their hands, they prayed
they sat silent in the sun, they waited
then they disappeared the first day
green rose from the ground

Canada, 2001

xxv

They lay down in long sweet arms,
in the deep scent of roots, they sang,
green fills all the paths, fills all
the paths in green, sweetgrass
and stargrass belong to earth,
to earth belong, fireweed
and milkweed fill all the paths, fill all
the paths in green.

It was all sighing and disclosing the night
the tide fell far back and the flower mouths
of anemones made wet sounds of small animals
drinking. They heard newborns calling. They found their way
to the island without a boat. They walked to the dry centre
where sea-animals slept shining. They saw the moon
release the weight of the world's water. They undressed
beside the dark-blue animals and danced.

Leda gathers ripe strawberries then stands smiling
in the doorway, lifting her stained hem upward.
Fruit flares in the wet pouch and they smell spring
and summer together. When they bite down,
the strawberries explode like stars
and in that moment they are more than
happy, they are set free.

4. Hannah's Letters Home

When you are a friend of God, fire is your water.
— Rumi

Listen, my friend, the heart is the road opening.
— Mirabai

i

Is it possible to see and stay intact? Being mad
we are in some sort of way holy, not sad.

It is the surprise of becoming a shy animal
again and seeing the world without clothing.

If left alone we could watch all day
what brightens and what darkens.

Nothing mediated. The pond illuminated the fish
when the late morning sun pierced them with heat.

We are blind to our own transparency
you once said. Noble friend, be my eyes.

ii

Is it possible to look into the world
and our own hearts at the same time?

Some days nothing is separate. Spring crocuses are acknowledged.
Letters answered.

The poppy seeds you sent last year rise surprised
as red light from hell and sing, *heaven, we're in heaven.*

Are saints necessary for salvation? I believe
no-one is saved and no-one is lost.

What isn't invented by the other? Tempered
in the slow rush of becoming?

iii

The whole world is inside of me and yet
I have lived as though I am only myself.

The feral cat eats from a bowl
cracked with grey threads.

He leaves food for the shy sister who has
one brown eye and one blurred blue.

Killer and almsgiver, he hunts in the garden,
leaps into sapphire air. Arcs

his body, a muscular doorway
the world rushes under.

iv

We are each other's raw material.
Fugitive weeds wild for story.

Watch that little boy chase the chickens,
each laughing in his own language.

All of it natural and necessary.
Look how lovely they are.

Any small child or animal leaping
for the sensation of leaping.

A curve in space.The way a cat suspends
for a long wild moment before landing.

v

The body remembers. It can learn to speak
without getting trapped in the telling.

When the dam in my throat opens its tiny blue gate,
birds nesting there will cry out and begin dreaming.

Without dreams, I don't know my own body,
there is no moon, no boat to begin again.

Old expectations that require mending the moon
dream departure.

Moving through. Memory of murder,
the vanished not so visceral.

vi

Hard to separate reading from sex,
sex from the sky, birds from the ocean,

blue from the heron. The unborn float
close to the dead. Those we know,

the chickens, the deer, relatives are
dreaming, arriving and leaving.

We used to take more time, swim all summer,
make love longer. We used to stay in the boat

sunrise to sunset. We used to mourn the dead
so the dead knew it.

vii

All summer small fires started,
combustions of conversation that left me weeping.

I aligned my sorrow with the sorrow of others
and now I can't tell right from left.

I am the one who strains to see the heartbeat
in the red tulip with the bright green stem.

The third one
who is bewildered.

There is a holy fire in each of us
and it is this burning we are most afraid of.

viii

Is a threshold a place where things are thrashed
and beaten apart? Is it a burning thing?

Distillation takes time. Dreams might disappear,
hearts might explode.

A constellation of stars singes the night.
My mind, sharp specks of fire, no wind.

I often worried about that light
tripping out and no breaker switch.

Like all fools I set fire
to the only house that sheltered me.

I could never let go of the shyness of being
seen, an undressing, dangerous and difficult.

How to stand here, human?
In trust, in trust, in trust.

I saw the feral cat sleeping in a secret summer palace
where the mint grows wild in the dry creek.

An apothecary for the mad and morose. A life
lived only as rational would be unbearable.

I mean what would you do
with an abundance of sunflowers?

x

The dream I want to undress but don't. It is
its own oracle: a life inside a life.

Your dream of sleeping free under the open sky
is illegal in this country but I know a place.

I am grateful for the stars,
how they saturate my body at night and breathe.

In this house of night vision
I slowly become awake.

Dreams shine in that place. A newborn
seeing the pulse of the world everywhere.

I practise Parker's thirteen keys of improvisation;
the liquid art of unlocking.

Borders bleed like the sea bleeds,
without stopping.

Blue becomes more blue and inside
a deeper shade of blue.

Leda's paintings for the unborn;
swimmers blinded by water.

Beatitudes of the mutable and the mundane.
I mean the blue dress I loved.

xii

I remember how you worked
in a silence concentrated as the sun;

how you opened the windows wide
and painted at least one room wisteria blue.

How many times did you reinvent a heart
that shaped itself into a room,

an ear that said,
I'm listening, I'm listening.

There is room for all
the sorrow, all the forgotten.

xiii

All week it was just me and six deer,
a silent solidarity.

Everything needed is here. A wholeness that language
denies, the way putting on clothes forgets nakedness.

If I am still, unimposing,
there is immense peace.

I am happy for the apples picked and pressed
that this morning hung by wooden threads.

An instinct, an aesthetic instinct for the ordinary
light in life, peaceful and delicately detached.

Bone and wood, spine against tree trunk.
Bark and vertebra, two bodies and in between.

This heart, what's me, what's you?
Solidarity isn't what's on the surface.

Everybody has a geography
grafted for grace.

Leda's paintings stand tall in my heart. Not a cliché,
the alders wrap limb around limb.

The trees lean, weep, breathe open
secrets. Weather is endless.

I live close to the small, the chickens, the cats,
the short walk to the creek.

And love the larger solitude,
the sea.

Lateral intelligence, a long, long river rejoicing.
How blue and red reshape our furious hearts.

The sea remembers. My half-human heart
with its imperfect words sends liquid letters.

Let's meet somewhere in transit.
We'll take the small blue boat.

About the Author

K. Louise Vincent was born in Pine Falls, Manitoba. As a community activist and therapist she devoted many years to social change and alternatives to violence rooted in feminist and non-violence ethics. She wrote *Transforming Abuse: Non-violent Resistance and Recovery*, published by New Society Press. Several of her poems have been published in literary journals and chapbooks, including *The Letter Poems* (written with Joanne Thorvaldson). K. Louise now lives on Gabriola Island.